Original title:
Living in the Walls of Home

Copyright © 2025 Creative Arts Management OÜ
All rights reserved.

Author: Elias Marchant
ISBN HARDBACK: 978-1-80587-181-1
ISBN PAPERBACK: 978-1-80587-651-9

Guardians of Shared Solitude

In a house where socks go to hide,
I trip over shoes like a clumsy guide.
The fridge hums tunes like a friend so sly,
While the cat plots schemes, oh my, oh my!

Veils of Everyday Life

The laundry dances, a colorful waltz,
Dust bunnies wiggle, we share their faults.
Coffee spills secrets on the morning floor,
As the toast pops up with a crack, not a score.

The Unseen Underbelly

Behind every couch, a treasure lies,
Old snacks and memories, oh what a prize!
The vacuum's a monster, a noisy beast,
Chasing crumbs like a hungry feast.

Flow of Time in Tight Spaces

Tick-tock, the clock gives a sly little grin,
As I search for my phone—I can't find it, again!
Walls echo laughter, like a warm embrace,
In this tiny kingdom, we all find our place.

The Quiet Bond of Walls

In the silent scheme of things,
Walls eavesdrop on all our flings.
They witness my dance in socks,
And my kitchen battles with the clocks.

The walls laugh at my clumsy falls,
As I trip over shoes and bouncy balls.
They've heard my secrets, my whispered dreams,
And they chuckle softly at my silly schemes.

Grains of Time Under One Roof

Tick tock goes the old grandfather clock,
While dust bunnies gather near the sock.
We share inside jokes with every tick,
The cat gives a sigh, she's seen my tricks.

We wake each day to the same old view,
Where cereal spills make humorous stew.
Mom finds spaghetti caked on the wall,
And we all burst out laughing at the fall.

Beyond the Entryway

Cross the threshold, welcome to chaos,
Where each room's a stage for the gloss.
In the living room, I'm queen of the mess,
With blankets and snacks, my kingdom I bless.

The hallway's a maze of today's dirty shoes,
A perilous journey, but what do I choose?
Will I wade through laundry or dodge the odd chair?
It's a fun little dance—should I even care?

The Pulse of the Every Day

Morning coffee with a side of cheer,
Creaky floors sing, 'Hey, come over here!'
I spill my dreams and some orange juice too,
Then chase a rogue cat who's taken my shoe.

Afternoon giggles fill the air,
As siblings engage in a hilarious dare.
The walls all quiver at our loud delight,
Keeping our secrets through every night.

The Heartbeat of Four Walls

In the kitchen, pots do dance,
Spices swirl, a fragrant prance.
The oven hums a merry tune,
While the fridge marks afternoons.

Couch cushions play hide and seek,
A remote lost during the week.
Dogs stare with a playful bark,
Wondering where the snacks embark.

Shadows leap when lights go out,
Echoed laughter, what's it about?
Pictures nod with silent cheer,
While chairs spin tales we all hold dear.

Memories Drift in Dusty Corners

Amidst the clutter, treasures hide,
Old board games waiting for a ride.
Dust bunnies tumble like midair flips,
While grandma's vase does a few skips.

Notes scribbled on faded tags,
Forgotten tales in crumpled rags.
Each corner whispers sweet old schemes,
Of summer nights and childhood dreams.

A sock here, a shoe lost there,
The laundry piles, a hearty scare.
Echoes shout of messy beds,
And stories spun in sleepy heads.

Secrets of the Stalwart Roof

On rafters high, where dustballs reign,
The echo of the rain's refrain.
Squirrels plotting their cheeky flight,
While pigeons honor rooftop height.

Chirping birds hold a daily chat,
With secrets wrapped in feathered hat.
Lightning bolts and thunder's roar,
Leave witness tales on every floor.

The attic's stash, a time capsule,
Old wedding hats, and granddad's tassel.
Whispers float through aged beams,
As the world outside bustles and dreams.

Patches of Light in Dimmed Rooms

Sunlight spills like liquid gold,
On dusty books that dare be bold.
Window curtains wave like flags,
In a battle of midday gags.

A cat naps in a sunlit patch,
While shadows play a little match.
Bouncing off walls with a grin,
As if to say, let the fun begin!

Each creak of floorboards laughs aloud,
While chairs recline, feeling proud.
The dance of light, a cheeky sight,
Turns every room to pure delight!

The Home That Holds Us

In every nook, a secret hides,
The cat pretends, on sunny sides.
The fridge hums songs of midnight snacks,
While socks play hide and seek, relax!

The doorbell rings, a surprise guest,
I check my hair, did I look best?
But they just come, to steal some bread,
While I roll my eyes, and keep my spread.

The ceiling fan spins tales untold,
Of shouting matches, brave and bold.
I laugh at memories stuck on replay,
From youth's wild antics, our silly play.

Each beam and corner knows our quirks,
Like running from chores, or playful jerks.
Here we create our funny script,
In this cozy place, forever gripped.

Beyond the Threshold of Dreams

Beyond the door, a kingdom waits,
With cereal spills and endless debates.
The couch, our throne, where we all sprawl,
In this grand realm, we're kings in the hall.

The dog wags tales of postman fear,
While masked in fluff, he rules the sphere.
Clothes on the floor, a mountain range,
Life's little quirks that never change.

The bathroom fights, for mirror space,
Grins and giggles, a chaotic race.
Kitchen dances, while we prep our feasts,
Where laughter roars, and worry's ceased.

Books stacked high, a leaning tower,
Every page drips with adventure's power.
In this wacky world, we find our groove,
In our silly dance, forever we move.

Silent Sentinels of Space

In the corner, a lamp stands tall,
With wobbly legs, it threatens to fall.
Its light flickers, softens the night,
Casting shadows, a comical sight.

The fridge hums a cheerful tune,
Dances under the light of the moon.
It swallows snacks in a greedy bite,
Popping open with a goofy delight.

Corners of Comfort

Cushions piled high, a soft, cozy throne,
Where the cat claims rights, in a sleepy tone.
It purrs like a motor, in dreamy repose,
While I search for the remote, well who really knows?

The dust bunnies gather, they host a grand ball,
In the quiet of corners, they're having a sprawl.
With tiny top hats, they dance on the floor,
As I sweep them up, they scatter for more.

Fragments of Family

A fridge note scribbled in vibrant crayon,
Declares love for pizza—but only for Saigon.
With each mumbled secret and giggles in pairs,
The echoes of children bounce off the stairs.

Mom's cooking up chaos, a recipe bold,
In a pot of confusion, the flavors unfold.
We feast on the laughter, mistakes that we own,
With crumbs on our faces, we're never alone.

Beneath the Roof's Embrace

The roof creaks a tune, a silly old song,
As squirrels scurry, where do they belong?
Beneath this shelter, we share our best jokes,
With laughter that echoes like old-fashioned folks.

Pajamas are worn like an everyday crown,
As I trip on my slippers and tumble right down.
In the midst of our chaos, we find room to play,
In this quirky abode, we laugh through the day.

Sheltered Whispers

In the nook where socks disappear,
Teddies giggle, 'Oh dear, oh dear!'
The cupboard's secret, stale cupcake,
Nibbled by mice who just want a break.

Echoes of laughter bounce off the walls,
Crumbs from cookies that someone recalls.
The floorboards creak, a dance of old,
While dust bunnies quietly plot and scold.

Echoes of Familiar Spaces

The fridge hums tunes, a serenade sweet,
While the toaster pops out a breakfast treat.
The cat runs circles, a champion spry,
Chasing shadows—oh my, oh my!

Old chairs creak like they've told the best tale,
Spilling secrets like a feisty snail.
Pictures giggle from the wall with flair,
Winking at visitors, if they dare!

Shadows Beneath the Eaves

Under the stairs, a monster lies still,
But all it wants is a good, big meal.
Half-empty snacks, and a single string,
A dust mote's dance—that's the best thing!

Around the corners where dust bunnies roam,
Whispers of mischief are found in each home.
Socks play hide and seek, never to match,
With the old clock ticking, our everyday catch!

Portraits of Our Quiet Nooks

Cushions stacked high like a royal throne,
Where pillows debate who's been overthrown.
A laundry pile, the leanest of peaks,
With a sock army that has their techniques.

The bathtub sings, a bubbly tune,
While rubber ducks float, chasing the moon.
The garden gnome nods, wise and aware,
Of all the oddities lost in thin air!

The Weight of Silence in the Air

In the quiet corners, dust bunnies leap,
Whispering secrets that we never keep.
The fridge hums a tune, its rhythm off beat,
While socks plot revenge, a laundry retreat.

The cat eyes the curtains, plotting a climb,
As we trip on the carpet, oh what a crime!
Laughter spills over like sauce on the floor,
In a house filled with echoes, who could ask for more?

Gossamer Threads of Familiarity

Coffee cups clink, a morning parade,
Each sip is a joke, in warmth we're arrayed.
Old chairs creak puns, their voices so sly,
As we all crack up, oh my, oh my!

The couch knows our tales, from grumbles to cheer,
It's swayed in the chaos, year after year.
Tangled up earbuds, a musical fight,
Yet somehow we dance in the dimming light.

Traces of Us in Every Room

The kitchen's a battlefield of crumbs and snacks,
While the dog hides the remotes, giving us flaks.
Stains on the wallpaper tell stories untold,
Of pizza night laughter, and antics so bold.

The bathroom mirror holds our sleepy grins,
Which toothbrush is whose? It's where the fun begins.
In hallways we stumble, on dreams maybe lost,
Collecting those moments, it's worth any cost.

A Tapestry of Echoing Footsteps

Each footsteps a echo, a symphony grand,
Chasing the cat, who thinks she's the band.
The stairs groan in laughter as we run by,
With socks full of holes, how hard we can fly!

Door hinges creak jokes when friends come to play,
While plants are the audience, in sun they sway.
With each little mishap, our hearts laugh resound,
In every nook, the joy we have found.

Enclaves of Heartfelt Reverie

In the nook of the couch where I sink,
A snack stashed away, quick as a wink.
The cat takes a throne, regal and grand,
While I hide my crumbs, quick with my hand.

The fridge hums a tune, a quirky delight,
As leftovers waltz in the soft fridge light.
I dance 'round the kitchen, a chef on a spree,
But burn my creation — oh, woe is me!

My socks are a pair, but they wander apart,
Declaring their freedom, a true work of art.
I chase after socks with a theatrical flair,
While the dog steals my snack, without any care.

These walls know my secrets, my laughter, my flaws,
Like a sitcom set, they embrace all my cause.
In this cozy abode, where both shadows play,
Life's a grand circus, I'm the clown every day.

Unfolding Stories in Every Cranny

There's a story tucked under my chair,
A mismatch of dust bunnies, oh what a pair!
They secretly plot as I sit with a grin,
Beneath the old furniture, chaos begins.

The curtains flap tales of sunbeams and dust,
A dance of the old, in the wind they trust.
Each fold hints of stories I'm yet to uncover,
About sock whispers and the cat's little blunders.

In the cupboard, surprises wait for my hand,
A cookie jar lurking, it's perfectly planned.
With stealth like a ninja, I raid with glee,
Beware of the kitchen if you want to see me!

Every corner's a portal to whimsical fun,
Where laughter erupts until the day done.
My home, a companion, a joyful retreat,
In this kaleidoscope life, I dance to the beat.

Masks of Warmth in the Chill of Winter

The thermostat's broken, it's freezing inside,
Blankets draped over like a cozy tide.
A thermos of cocoa becomes my warm friend,
While I float through the rooms, snuggled 'til the end.

The firewood piles up as the snow starts to fall,
It's a game of 'who's coldest?'—come one, come all!
We build a fortress of pillows and sheets,
In the fortress of warmth, we huddle for feats!

With socks that are mismatched, I'm fashionably bold,
As I shuffle through drifts, feeling feisty and old.
Hot soup in my belly, I refuse to budge,
And on winter's frigid breath, I just won't judge!

The laughter erupts amid tales spun anew,
With tales of my slippers that never fit true.
In this cocoon of joy, I'm snug as can be,
Masked by warmth, it's a winter jubilee!

Rituals Bound by the Ceiling's Reach

Every evening's a challenge — who's dish is this?
With forks pointing at me, how could I resist?
The dinner table's circus, everyone's on stage,
As we banter and bicker like players in rage.

The socks on the line tell a tale of their own,
While I wave goodbye as they dance to be flown.
Laundry's a monster, but I'll take it in stride,
With a spin of the tale, I'm the laundry's guide!

In the corners, we gather for games of pure chance,
Hiding my giggles, I sneak in a glance.
Every board game a riot, every rule's up for grabs,
Dares and alliances, with the best of the jabs.

These rituals attract all the charm in each nook,
Where the ceiling's a witness to plans that we cook.
Home is a playground where laughter won't cease,
In this comedic abode, we carve our own peace.

The Quiet Alarm Clock of Routine

Each morning my sock hides away,
Behind the couch, it loves to play.
I chase it down with sleepy eyes,
While breakfast burns—oh, what a surprise!

The cat now dances on the floor,
He's found a spot—he needs no more.
With every stretch, the curtains sway,
My coffee's brewing, hip-hip-hooray!

The clock ticks loud, but I don't care,
I'll start my day with messy hair.
The toast pops up, a crispy delight,
And I'm still half-asleep, what a sight!

In this routine, I find the fun,
The loud alarm clock—I'm always on the run!
With socks and toast as my best friends,
This silly cycle never ends!

Whispers of Dawn and Dusk

The sun peeks in, it starts to shout,
The coffee machine makes me pout.
I wave goodbye to sleep's warm embrace,
Then trip on my cat—oh, what a race!

At dusk, the dishes growl and moan,
They whisper secrets I can't disown.
With every clank, my patience wears,
But the laughter sneaks in, no more cares!

Neighbors' lights twinkle like stars,
Their laughter mingles with my own jars.
In twilight's glow, we all collide,
With snacks and jokes, no need to hide!

So here we dance, from dawn to night,
In whispered tones, we find our light.
This funny chaos is where I'm home,
In quiet moments, I gladly roam!

Timeless Under the Eaves

The eaves above, they crack and creak,
With tales of dust and joy, so unique.
Each rain-dropped whisper bends my ear,
As I grab a snack and shift my gear.

Beneath the roof, the stories bloom,
Of socks misplaced and a hidden broom.
A game of hide-and-seek with time,
I laugh it off with a wacky rhyme!

When neighbors clash like thunderous pride,
I giggle loud, no need to hide.
With every conflict, humor will reign,
In this timeless spot, we'll dance again!

So here we dwell, with laughter near,
In every corner—a joke, a cheer.
With life so funny, I feel so free,
Under these eaves, it's all just me!

Foundations of Fear and Comfort

Beneath the stairs, a shadow lurks,
I fear it's where the dust-bunny works.
But when I peek with bated breath,
I find a treasure instead of death!

The fridge hums loud, it's quite a tune,
A symphony played by the midnight moon.
With snacks in hand, I gleefully tread,
The comfort found where I once fled!

In every nook, the echoes play,
Fears fade fast when silliness stays.
The laughter builds on shaky ground,
In this odd house, pure joy is found!

So may the shadows dance around,
In this funny fortress, I am bound.
With fear and comfort intertwined,
This crazy home is truly mine!

Silhouettes Against the Sunset

Cats chase shadows, light a game,
Puppies bark at suns that wane.
Lamps flicker as the laughter grows,
While wild socks dance in lazy toes.

Dinner's brewing with a scent so sweet,
Yet hidden dishes still face defeat.
The chair squeaks, it's found a voice,
Even plants seem to rejoice!

Jokes ricochet 'neath the ceiling gray,
And curtains sway as if to play.
In moments filled with endless glee,
Home holds secrets, just wait and see!

Sunsets fade, but the laughter stays,
In this crazy home, we've found our ways.

Cracks in the Paint

The wall knows whispers of days gone by,
Frosted flakes scream more than a pie.
A creaky floor with tales to share,
Echoes of mischief, everywhere!

A painting hangs slightly askew,
Its wonky smile is hard to view.
Don't mention that toilet seat's squeak,
It's a game of 'hide and don't seek!'

Chips in the plaster mark time's race,
While loose tiles wear a silly face.
In every nook, a story hides,
By the fridge, where the snack time bides!

And with laughter, we fix the cracks,
With humor as glue, there's no lack!

Patterns of Presence

Socks mismatched, a playful show,
In our little circus, on they go!
Pancakes flipped in a pan too small,
Create a breakfast, a sticky ball.

Books stacked high, a candid tower,
While time ticks by, we laugh for hours.
A rogue cat leaps on the random chair,
Statuesque joys fill the air!

Butterflies chase shadows that flit,
As family memories find their wit.
With every tick-tock and playful cheer,
Home paints a dance of love so clear!

Colors blend in a joyous maze,
Patterns formed in all our days.

Heartbeats Within These Walls

The fridge hums soft, like a lullaby,
As food disappears, and we all sigh.
Heartbeats echo in a mischievous tune,
Underneath the glow of a cheeky moon.

Laundry piles are mountains of cheer,
'Where's my other sock?' the question is clear.
In every corner, we find our space,
As giggles bounce at a frantic pace!

Plates stack high, a balancing act,
With each clink, it's a laugh-packed pact.
The walls embrace all our silly schemes,
Welcoming dreams wrapped in seams.

Every heartbeat a drum in this home,
With joy and chaos, we freely roam!

Stories in Each Brick

Each brick whispers tales of old,
Of sneezes, spills, and secrets told.
The cat has its throne, on top of the chair,
Watching the world with a regal glare.

Socks disappear, they play hide and seek,
Behind the couch, they give quite a tweak.
The dust bunnies dance, a little parade,
In our cozy fortress, where chaos is made.

Every corner holds laughter's embrace,
While shadows keep up in the silly race.
The fridge hums a tune, so out of tune,
While the walls share jokes that make us swoon.

Let's toast to the stories that fill every crack,
With each little quirk, there's nothing we lack.
In this friendly riot, we thrive and we bloom,
In our lively castle, there's always more room.

The Nesting Place

In the nesting place where we all reside,
With voices bouncing, there's nowhere to hide.
The pots and pans join in with their clatter,
Making a symphony—oh, what's the matter?

The broomstick dances, sweeping the floor,
While I chase the kids who burst through the door.
Each doodle on paper tells a tale anew,
In our home sweet home, where giggles ensue.

Tea spills on the table, patterned with glee,
While stories unfurl like a sail on the sea.
The clocks tick and tock, but we're never late,
In the nesting place, we revel in fate.

So grab a seat and let's share a laugh,
Life's little oddities—they fill the path.
With a quirky nature, this home is a poem,
In the nesting place, it's a fun zone to roam.

Where Memories Linger

Where memories linger, the walls come alive,
With echoes of laughter and fun to survive.
The shoes at the door, they tell their own tale,
Of muddy adventures and paths we sail.

The kitchen's a theater, with pots as the cast,
Where cookies are burnt but good times are vast.
We dance with the broom, with the radio loud,
In the place where the silly feels perfectly proud.

The bath mat's a stage for the splash and the giggle,
As rubber ducks waddle and little hearts wiggle.
Every corner is filled with a goofy squeak,
In this loving abode, where chaos is chic.

So gather around, let's spin tales from our past,
In this joyful retreat, where memories last.
With walls that support our quirks and our whims,
Life's a hilarious dance—with all of its grins.

Frames of Familiarity

Frames of familiarity hang on the wall,
Each picture a story, each smile is a call.
The cat in a bow tie, the dog wearing specs,
Mom doing the dance with two left feet flexed.

Socks strewn about, and crumbs in the chair,
Every day's treasure, our little affair.
The clock mocks our rhythm, it ticks with a grin,
While the walls roll their eyes at the mess we're in.

The remote is a ghost, it loves to hide,
In the couch's deep crevices, it takes a ride.
Popcorn spills over, a playful cascade,
In this frame of familiarity, memories are made.

So let's raise a glass to the funny and bright,
In frames of familiarity, there's pure delight.
With laughter as glue, we'll stick through it all,
In our quirky abode, we're having a ball.

The Space Between Us

In this small room, I search for snacks,
But my cat's got plans, she's plotting attacks.
Socks on the floor, a fortress of fluff,
Where I once had peace, now it's all just tough.

I tell my kid, please keep it down,
But they're mixing potions, wearing a crown.
The walls echo back their wild, loud screams,
I'm rethinking my dreams of quiet, it seems.

Under the table, a treasure I'll find,
Half-eaten cookies and crumbs intertwined.
What happened to order? It's lost in the fray,
Here's to the chaos, it's just our own way.

So raise up your glasses to disorderly fun,
This house is a circus, but we're on the run.
With giggles and wiggles, life is a race,
Embrace all the mayhem, it's our happy place!

Quietude of the Hearth

A mug of hot cocoa, the cats are aglow,
They're plotting their takeovers, a feline row.
While I seek peace, they leap and they fight,
In the cozy chaos, is that a new height?

The fireplace crackles, as socks start to fly,
With a rebel cheer, my pizza goes by.
The couch is a jungle, with pillows as fort,
While I make my escape, the snacks I'll deport.

Moments of silence, we cherish them dear,
But watch for the puppy—he's sneaking up near.
He's bilingual, a master of barks and of whines,
While I try to nap, he's making the signs.

So let's raise a toast to our hectic life crew,
Where joyful explosions are never asked to subdue.
With laughter and love, oh what a bright spark,
Even strained quietude feels like a lark!

Tapestry of Tenures

In my own room, I'm a queen, it's true,
But the laundry monster threatens my view.
Each sock forgotten, a tale left untold,
Turns into a legend, where critters grow bold.

The dust bunnies gather for their covert meets,
Plotting a coup on my clean kitchen sheets.
My coffee goes missing, my spoon joins the fray,
In this war of the mundane, it's survival play.

Toiletries rebel, they've staged their great fight,
In the depths of the cabinet, out of pure spite.
As I search for the toothpaste, it vanished—oh dear!
Guess it's another day of chaotic cheer.

So welcome the clutter, the highs, and the lows,
As we twirl through the madness, the laughter just flows.
In a home filled with warmth, where the antics won't stop,

Every day is a party, come join on the hop!

Remnants of Silent Laughter

Late-night whispers, we plot and we scheme,
With shadows for company, and ice cream supreme.
Jammies a-flap, as we dash to the fridge,
While the cat does a ballet atop the small ridge.

The hallway's a maze, with toys as our traps,
We zigzag and jump, through a sea of mishaps.
The laughter erupts, the dog gives a bark,
As we dance through the darkness, igniting a spark.

Each tumble and slip feels like comedy gold,
As we navigate chaos, the antics unfold.
So gather the moments, they're tiny but bright,
In this tapestry woven, let's bask in our light.

With remnants of laughter echoing near,
Our hearts feel at home, and we whistle, not fear.
In the midst of this mess, there's joy by the mile,
In our house of adventures, we're all in style!

Comfort Woven into Every Plank

In the corner, the cat lays flat,
Sprawled like a king on a welcome mat.
Chasing dust motes in a sunbeam's glow,
Plotting world takeovers, but moving slow.

Cushions piled high, a fort for the day,
With laughter and snacks barely kept at bay.
The fridge hums tunes, a symphony sweet,
While socks stage a dance to a beat complete.

The walls whisper secrets of meals gone by,
And family stories that make you cry.
Silly moments etched in every nook,
The joy of the familiar found in each book.

A light flickers once, and shadows parade,
As popcorn pop-dances, a home glade.
Through every giggle and every sigh,
The spirit of comfort will never die.

Treasures Tucked Beneath the Stairs

What's that lurking behind the old shoe?
A monster? Or maybe a snack left for two?
Forgotten treasures in the dust's embrace,
Like a half-eaten sandwich in a secret place.

Old toys with stories lie quiet and meek,
Crispy wrappers from snacks once unique.
The vacuum cleaner coughs in surprise,
At the socks it finds, living in disguise.

A runaway marble rolls under the light,
Bouncing and giggling, a cheeky delight.
The ghost of a dog with a wagging tail,
Chasing his dreams through a forgotten trail.

Beneath the stairs, a world to explore,
With echoes of laughter and tales to implore.
Grab your treasure map, an adventure awaits,
In the land of odd socks and cardboard crates.

Nestled Dreams in Forgotten Spaces

Up on the shelf, where old books reside,
Dusty pages hide tales of a ride.
A dragon once flew with a brave little knight,
Now trapped in the closet, they dream through the night.

The attic's a circus, with boxes galore,
The past juggles laughter while peeking through doors.
Magical trinkets like marbles and hats,
Hold gigs and whispers of old-fashioned chats.

In corners, the cobwebs gather and spin,
Stitching together the tales held within.
Where daydreams and night schemes dance hand in hand,

Creating a kingdom all perfectly planned.

So lift up the dust with a chuckle and cheer,
For a journey to laughter lies waiting near.
In every crevice, there's magic, you see,
In the hidden spots, wild and fancy-free.

Remnants of Time between Spaces

Between the walls, echoes of cheer,
In every sound, a story so dear.
A plunk of a spoon, a call to the meal,
Where memories linger and hearts start to feel.

The fridge plays tunes of leftovers past,
Reciting old dinners that went by too fast.
A chair creaks and groans like a stage in a show,
As laughter and giggles drift high and low.

From curtains that dance in the breeze's full swing,
To whispers of secrets the home likes to bring.
Faded snapshots stuck to the wall,
With winks and pouts, they silently call.

A tick of the clock marks the time that we've spent,
Moments so rich, they shimmer and bent.
In every small glitch and all the misplaced,
Is a snapshot of joy, still eternally chased.

Cadence of Domestic Life

In the kitchen, pots all dance,
A spatula's waltz, a fork's prance.
The toaster hums a cheerful tune,
While all the crumbs gather like a platoon.

The fridge sings low, a frosty song,
As leftovers claim their rights—so wrong.
The cat leaps high, a fluffy sprite,
Chasing shadows 'til the fall of night.

In the bathroom, rubber ducks float,
Having a party, singing a note.
The showerhead gurgles, quite offbeat,
As soap suds join in, a bubbly treat.

And so we twirl through this home affair,
Laughter echoes in the fresh, crisp air.
Each corner brews its little jest,
In this place, we all know best.

The Hidden Architecture of Affection

Under the couch, the socks convene,
Plotting escapes, places unseen.
They scheme and dream of the great outdoors,
While the dog snores loud, ignoring their roars.

In the hallway, picture frames clash,
Each smile a giggle, a silly splash.
While dust bunnies grow to epic sizes,
They plan their next move, hoping for surprises.

The pantry whispers secrets of snacks,
Crackers and cookies plotting their attacks.
With every crinkle of a chip bag sound,
It's a party of crunch that knows no bound.

And as we bustle through daily routine,
This architecture builds what can't be seen.
Jokes hide in drawers, warmth under the bed,
In a house where love's laughter is widely spread.

Silent Conversations of the Home

The walls listen close to every word,
A gossiping corner, haven for stirred.
Where the couch sees all, its cushions tight,
It's a soft throne for our laughter and slight.

The kitchen tiles hold secrets so bold,
With recipes marked in stories retold.
Even the cupboard, with a creak and a sigh,
Will whisper back tales as days slip by.

The hallway echoes with tiny feet,
Chasing dreams and breakfast treats.
The living room leans in for a chat,
As the cat critiques each human spat.

And in the night, when all is still,
The house breathes softly, a gentle thrill.
We share our thoughts in silence profound,
In this little nest, where love is found.

The Language of Dust

In corners, dust bunnies hold court,
Discussing the day's most thrilling report.
They tumble and twirl, in light's gentle beam,
While we vacuum them up, ruining their dream.

On shelves, layers form with every year,
A history told, yet none appear near.
Old trophies sit with stories undone,
While the stale air sneezes—'achoo!'—just for fun.

The windowsill listens, wide-eyed and dear,
Collecting whispers year after year.
As we open wide, let fresh air swoop,
It giggles aloud, a joyful whoop!

Oh dust, you crafty, light-hearted muse,
In your fluffy realms, we happily lose.
You teach us the joy in what's small and slight,
This home, our playground, from morning to night.

A Symphony of Soft Footfalls

Tiptoe around with squeaky shoes,
The floorboards protest, they love to snooze.
A dance on linoleum, the cat's in play,
Watch out for the vacuum, it's on today!

Pillow forts towering, a fortress so grand,
Watch as I command my stuffed animal band.
Duck tape my dreams, superhero cape,
In this cozy kingdom, there's no escape!

Sneaking snacks from the pantry, oh what a sin,
Crumbs on my shirt, let the game begin.
With each crinkled chip, a crunch that betrays,
Maybe mom won't notice? I hope she just stays!

The backyard's a jungle, my quest takes flight,
Exploring the wild till the fall of night.
Imagining kingdoms beneath the old stairs,
Here in my castle, adventure declares!

The Architecture of Us

In the living room, my throne made of fluff,
Remote in my hand, I can get rather tough.
Snack ninja skills, stealth mode is a must,
Between couch cushions, in crumbs I trust.

The kitchen's a science lab, recipes gone wild,
Mixing and stirring, not so mild.
The blender roars like a dragon at night,
As I dance around in my culinary fight!

Staircase to nowhere, a slide when I run,
Gravity's a partner, oh what fun!
A tumble and roll, laughter on cue,
Gravity's our friend, but let's keep it true.

Windows open wide, let the breeze take a chance,
Singing out loud, like I'm ruling a dance.
Neighbors chuckle, they think it's a show,
But this is our stage, here I'm the pro!

Reflection in the Broken Glass

The mirror plays tricks, my hair's in a whirl,
A masterpiece daubed, in every curl.
The past me is smiling, or is that just me?
Laugh lines like maps lead to joy and glee.

Splattered paint and cereal bowls collide,
Messy art projects I'll never hide.
Balloons in the hallway, a floating parade,
This home is a circus, each day never strayed.

Footprints on walls, like art from a child,
The spirit of laughter remains undefiled.
Tagging the fridge, sort of an athlete,
In the gallery of goodness, my heart skips a beat!

Self-portraits from yesterday, scribbled with flair,
Who drew that, hmm? A masterpiece rare!
With a wink and a giggle, I claim my domain,
It's all in good fun — no need to explain!

Our Own Private Echo Chamber

Chatter and giggles bounce off the walls,
Echoes of chaos where laughter enthralls.
The sound of my sneakers, a stampede on stairs,
Each creak is a symphony, no room for cares.

Mimicking voices, I'm a parrot today,
Bouncing off walls, in a silly display.
The air's thick with antics, we're a silly troupe,
Bring on the fun in this homey soup!

Socks on the ceiling? It's a fashion surprise,
My wardrobe's a comedy, in a home of goodbyes.
The doorbell's a tune, we answer with flair,
Twirling and whirling, spirits in the air!

Telling tall tales with each little crack,
In the echo chamber, there's no looking back.
We're a riot of chuckles, a band of delight,
In this wacky abode, everything feels right!

Hearthside Reveries

Upon the couch, I sip my tea,
While socks and cats join company.
The clock strikes noon, a cat parade,
As crumbs collect and laughter's made.

The fridge hums tunes of fridge delights,
Exploring snacks on lazy nights.
Dancing spoons in kitchen's glow,
We spin and twirl, with snacks in toe.

Remote control, my wand of fate,
Texting snacks to elevate.
Couch cushions hold my secret dreams,
And all is well, or so it seems.

The world outside may howl and bite,
But here my heart can take its flight.
With every giggle and slight slip,
Life's just a goofy little trip.

Sheltered from the Storm

Raindrops drumming on the roof,
As we bounce around, quite aloof.
With blankets piled in a cozy mound,
We're explorers of this warm, safe ground.

The vacuum roars like a beast untamed,
As we hide and seek, unashamed.
With laundry piles like mountain peaks,
We laugh at dress codes, not unique.

Soup's on simmer, a fragrant delight,
While socks agree to join the fight.
Pillow forts rise, our castle's grand,
In this tiny kingdom, we take a stand.

So let it rain and wind those gales,
Our laughter dances, it never fails.
Wrapped in warmth, we boldly cheer,
For storms just swirl, we have no fear.

The Unbroken Circle

Round the dinner table, stories fly,
While pasta spins and laughter's high.
Spilled juice becomes a work of art,
In this circle, love's the best part.

Mom's loud jokes that steal the show,
Grandpa's tales, a wandering flow.
With every bite of pie we share,
This circle grows, love fills the air.

The dog's underfoot, a sneaky thief,
As crumbs cascade, it's no relief.
We giggle as he makes his play,
In this joyful game, we stake our stay.

With every hug and playful shove,
In this circle, we find our love.
Though foods may spill, and guests come late,
In our hearts, this bond is great.

The Color of Familiarity

The walls are dressed in a pastel glow,
As socks parade in colors flow.
Fridges hum a soft refrain,
While echoes dance like friendly rain.

With posters peeling, moments freeze,
In comfy chairs, we share our cheese.
The coffee spills, a very close friend,
In this sweet chaos, smiles don't end.

Remote in hand, we channel surf,
Making choices with joyful mirth.
We laugh at reruns, oh so old,
In this cocoon, we're brave and bold.

Familiar scents weave through the air,
Each corner whispers love and care.
In colors bright and laughter's tune,
Our home is painted with a funny boon.

Guardian Encounters

A sock floats by, defying the floor,
It's clearly a ghost who just loves to explore.
My cat takes aim, with a twitch of her tail,
Yet the sock escapes, while I laugh without fail.

The fridge hums softly, a comforting tune,
While the leftovers plot to escape with the moon.
Each time I approach, they sigh and they groan,
As though they've conspired to claim the throne.

The toaster pops up with a joyful surprise,
As crumbs celebrate like confetti in the skies.
"Not again!" I chuckle, "You crumbly beast!"
But buddies in chaos make breakfast a feast.

With walls that can giggle and floors that can dance,
Each nook and each cranny deserves a chance.
To conjure up laughter from every odd spot,
In this house of mischief, joy is the plot.

Nature's Reverberation Inside

A plant looks up, with a stalk so tall,
Whispers to curtains as they sway and sprawl.
The spider spins tales in threads oh so fine,
While I serve as the audience, sipping on wine.

The windows creak softly, joining in song,
As rain starts to tap, 'Is this where I belong?'
The couch seems to giggle, embracing the chill,
Inviting me close for a cozy goodwill.

An apple rolls slowly, it's seeking some fun,
On the table it bounces, oh what a run!
If fruit could converse, I'd say they conspired,
To give me a laugh, not one I desired.

The clock on the wall ticks in cheeky delight,
Counting each moment, then sleeps through the night.
In this indoor jungle where chaos can bloom,
Even stillness joins in, creating a room.

The Sheltered Whimsy

A cushion retreats, it's lost in a binge,
As socks gather round, they concoct a fringe.
The remote is a king, in his soft velvet throne,
While we bow to the screen, never left alone.

My shoes form a huddle, what secrets they keep,
Whispering stories as I drift off to sleep.
Each tangled shoelace has a tale of its own,
Maybe it's happy that it's finally grown.

Pillows hold meetings, both lofty and plush,
With giggles and whispers they banter and hush.
If walls could just talk, oh the stories they'd share,
Of the antics that linger in the evening air.

The ceiling fan twirls with a mischievous flair,
As lightbulbs exchange glances, crumbs in their hair.
In this realm of whimsy, delight blooms so bright,
Even furniture shares in the joyful delight.

Hidden Corners of Contentment

In a corner, a book sneezes, dust takes a leap,
As bookmarks embark on a journey of sleep.
Every page turns softly, with secrets to tell,
Of battles and voyages, like a magical spell.

The corners conspire to hide all my snacks,
While my dog gives chase to imaginary tracks.
With a woof and a wag, he pounces with glee,
As shadows retreat, from his playful decree.

The light flickers gently, a beacon in tune,
As plants hold their breath and summon the moon.
On the rug, I see laughter painted in threads,
As cushions conspire to cushion my heads!

These walls hold a treasure, where mirth runs so wild,
A dance of joy echoes, like a curious child.
In nooks and in crannies, delight swirls around,
In hidden corners of joy, my heart is unbound.

Warmth Within Closed Doors

The cat's on the table, it's taking a nap,
While I steal a cookie, oh what a trap!
Socks mismatched dancing, a sight to behold,
In this cozy chaos, our stories unfold.

The dog thinks he's human, sits on the chair,
Wearing a sweater, he jumps in the air!
Laughter erupts as the jokes go around,
In our funny little kingdom, love knows no bounds.

The fridge hums a tune, cries for a snack,
While the plants plot their takeover - watch your back!
The walls go on gossiping, secrets they keep,
In this warm little bubble, we all dive deep.

Here, every corner holds memories bright,
From dance party mishaps to tickle fights light.
With quirks and with chuckles, our home is a jest,
In the warmth of these walls, we truly are blessed.

The Symphony of Stillness

In this awkward silence, we share the space,
The clock's ticking loudly, it's lost in the race.
A sneeze breaks the stillness, we all turn around,
Is it a solo or a deep, muffled sound?

The fridge door swings open, a friendly old tune,
While spoons and forks gather like a raucous commune.
Each creaky old floorboard joins in the fun,
In our orchestra of stillness, we're never outdone.

Pet goldfish are gossiping under the peak,
As the couch makes a comment about our next week.
The chair squeaks in laughter, the table agrees,
As we moan and we groan, we're all just at ease.

So here's to the quiet, the laughter so sly,
As whispers and echoes drift by with a sigh.
In the symphony of moments, we find our own tune,
In this home of stillness, our hearts are attuned.

Threads of Togetherness

With mismatched socks and spaghetti stains bright,
We gather like stitches, in warmth and delight.
Crazy stories tumble, from tongue to the floor,
In our patchwork of laughter, always wanting more.

A dance in the kitchen, we twirl with glee,
As the dog chases bubbles. Oh look at him flee!
Mom's cooking a riot, spices all collide,
In our fabric of joy, no need to hide.

Napping on couches, like pillows we lean,
Each sneeze that erupts is a comedic scene.
With threads intertwined, the fabric is thick,
In our tapestry woven, life's magic will stick.

So here's to the moments that make us feel whole,
In this quirky abode, we nourish the soul.
Together we stitch every day into gold,
In this quilt of togetherness, stories unfold.

Imprints of the Past

Old photos are scattered, like breadcrumbs of yore,
Memories materialize, knocking at the door.
A sock puppet's grinning, from the shelf up above,
With each silly story, we're wrapped up in love.

The creaky old staircase whispers tales to our feet,
Of trips with high giggles, and one messy feat.
Each mark on the wall is a badge of a fight,
Where we tussled with pillows in the warm evening light.

The memories squeak like our favorite chair,
As bedtime stories echo through soft evening air.
From spaghetti disasters to grandpa's old hat,
Every pop of the clock holds a moment like that.

So here in these moments, we gather the gleam,
With laughter and stories, we all chase the dream.
In the imprints of time, we forever will play,
In this quirky old home, come what may.

Light Through the Panes

Sunbeams sneak in, warm and bright,
Chasing dust bunnies into flight.
Socks on the floor, a colorful spree,
In this game of hide and seek, just me!

The cat eyes a shadow with great intent,
While toast pops up, a breakfast event.
A dance of crumbs on the floor I see,
As I munch and laugh, just my friends and me.

Portraits of Stillness

The walls hold secrets, tales set to roam,
A portrait of chaos feels just like home.
Mom's slippers go missing, where could they be?
A desperate search, oh, where is that spree?

A remote control, it's a legendary quest,
Who hid it this time? It's a family jest!
Lost in the cushions, it sends us to glee,
For every small chaos, brings joy to the spree.

Gentle Echoes of Yesterday

Echoes of laughter in every room,
Like ghosts of the past creating a bloom.
A sock on the ceiling, how did it fly?
I bet it was grandpa, oh my, oh my!

The fridge hums a tune, a symphonic delight,
While leftovers waltz in the dim kitchen light.
The pantry's a treasure, both silly and sweet,
Each snack a reminder of home's tasty treat.

Nooks of Nostalgia

In the nook by the window, I sip and I sigh,
The cat's curled beside me, it's just us and pie.
Old stories spill out, like ketchup in jars,
Quirky recounts and distant memoirs.

Licorice whips, we throw 'em up high,
Splats on the wall, oh, how we do try!
In memory's haven, we laugh and we roll,
Each nook a warm hug, it captures the soul.

Echoes in the Halls

In the hall, I hear my cat,
Chasing shadows, imagine that!
Walls whisper tales of who did roam,
Where's the pizza? Oh, I miss home!

Underneath the kitchen sink,
A monster lurks, or so I think.
But wait, it's just a sock mislaid,
Dance with me, before it fades!

The creaky stairs begin to groan,
Is it the house, or just my own?
Each little sound, a lively tune,
I swear, they laugh at me at noon!

Hide and seek with ghosts so bright,
They play in shadows, day and night.
I planted dreams in every crack,
With every echo, there's no lack!

The Heartbeat of Four Walls

Every corner tells a joke,
A secret shared with every poke.
My fridge hums, a symphony,
Of leftover forks and mystery!

The couch is king, it takes its seat,
Roaring laughter, and then retreat.
Remote controls always on strike,
A battle fought with every hike!

In the bathroom, a rubber duck,
Float around with luck, oh what luck!
Echoes bounce off every tile,
Makes me giggle, stay awhile!

The windows frame the world outside,
Where breezes dance with joy and pride.
Here in my fortress, love prevails,
Through joyful sighs and playful trails!

Secrets Encased in Plaster

Behind the wall, a riddle hides,
Maybe it's truth, or just my guides.
Dust bunnies hold the house's lore,
Turning every day to a chore!

Underneath the bed, it seems,
Live all the socks of crazy dreams.
Where's my left shoe? Oh, dear me!
It danced away, not meant to be!

Pictures crooked on the wall,
Laughing faces, having a ball.
Every frame a tale or two,
Of silly moments shared by you!

The mantelpiece, a dusty stage,
For all the antics of this age.
I raise a toast, here's to the mess,
In every crack, oh, what a jest!

Breath of the Household

The kitchen sings, oh pots and pans,
Creating music, dance with hands.
A blender roars, a chef's delight,
Until the milk takes off in flight!

Laundry dances, clothes on a spree,
Round and round, just wait and see.
A dryer hums a cozy tune,
In socks and shirts, I'll dance till noon!

Every creak brings a timely jest,
My sneaker squeaks, I feel so blessed.
With laughter ringing through the air,
This joyous place, beyond compare!

The heartbeat thumps as we all play,
In this abode, come what may.
Together here, with love we throng,
In every corner, we all belong!

Tones of Togetherness

In a house where laughter roams,
Socks mismatched, but still like home.
Cooking fails and kitchen cheers,
Echoes of our joyful years.

Cats invade the cozy chair,
Plotting schemes beyond our care.
Coffee spills and sticky floors,
Dance-off battles, open doors.

Off-key tunes from bathroom tunes,
A chorus born of nowhere, loons.
We sing in harmony, just a bit,
Our family love is truly lit.

Amid the chaos, hugs unite,
In this space, we find delight.
Messy, silly, never bland,
Together always, hand in hand.

Unfolding Stories Behind Each Door

Knock-knock jokes from the hallway bright,
Secrets whispered late at night.
Behind each door, a tale unfolds,
In laughter, love, and stories told.

Sibling feuds over the remote,
Who lost the game? No one will gloat.
A tripping hazard on the floor,
Every bump a laugh to explore.

Tick-tock echoes of the clock,
Parental sighs, a playful mock.
The fridge hums a silly tune,
While we plot our capers, every afternoon.

In every corner, memories clung,
Where all are welcome, tales are sung.
Like dusty books on a shelf so grand,
Every story woven, hand in hand.

Pockets of Peace

In a nook where blankets lie,
Sunshine spills like sweet goodbye.
A corner where the cat sprawls wide,
Peace of mind, a joyful ride.

Amidst the chaos, calm we find,
In whispered words, hearts aligned.
Tea brews slow, the kettle sings,
Here, life feels like gentler things.

Mismatched cushions, pillows galore,
A kingdom built on the living room floor.
In cozy chaos, we take a seat,
Togetherness makes our world complete.

Laughter bubbles over the hum,
In our little pocket, bliss is spun.
Huddled close, we share our dreams,
In this sanctuary, life redeems.

Shelter for the Soul

Four walls, a roof, and quirky sights,
Here we gather, in silly bites.
Beneath the rooftop, chaos hums,
Our shelter sings with fun and drums.

The living room, a circus ring,
With misplaced shoes and a dog that sings.
Forgotten snacks and couch potato pride,
In this madness, joy can't hide.

Family meetings turn to jest,
We argue, and we laugh, the best.
In pockets of time, we find our role,
This place, dear friends, is our heart's control.

Crafting memories, day by day,
In this haven, we tumble and sway.
A warm embrace, a funny stroll,
In every corner, a shelter for the soul.

Passages of Time Held in Frame

In the hallway, a clock ticks loud,
Counting moments, it feels quite proud.
Cats chase dust, like tiny meteors,
While I sip tea and ponder my chores.

Frames hold faces, all grinning wide,
Some come to visit, others just hide.
Photographs laughter, in blissful refrain,
While I wonder if I can dance in the rain.

Socks on the stairs, a masquerade ball,
Everyone's waltzing, I'm stuck in the hall.
The dog steals my snack, a comical heist,
As I clutch my cookies, so desperate, so nice.

Time flows like syrup, thick as can be,
Yet in this snug space, there's always a spree.
So let's toast to the chaos, the giggles and gaffes,
Wrapped in our stories, mishaps, and laughs.

Sanctuaries of Solitude and Togetherness

In the kitchen, I craft a fine stew,
While the kids throw flour – who knew they could stew?
Each spoonful's a battle, a taste test affair,
And the dog's on standby, ready to share.

The living room's ripe with popcorn fights,
As movies flicker on cozy nights.
Cushions are forts; we're kings and queens,
In a kingdom of laughter and goofy scenes.

Bubbles in the bathroom rise like a show,
Rubber duckies chorus, "You won't want to go!"
While I seek solace in a five-minute soak,
Life's scattered confetti, warmth, and a joke.

Evenings find us, huddled in a heap,
Family stories are ours to keep.
Between giggles and sighs, we dance through the day,
In our sanctuary, where love's here to stay.

Whispers Beneath the Floorboards

Beneath the floor, the critters convene,
Plotting mischief, unseen and serene.
They gossip at night, while we're fast asleep,
A symphony of squeaks, their secrets run deep.

Toys come alive, and so does the dust,
In the corners they gather, oh, it's a must!
The vacuum goes rogue; they scatter and flee,
While I just stare, sipping my tea.

Every creak tells a story, a squeak and a sigh,
Of old shoes and games, of kites that could fly.
Underneath, the whispers sparkle with glee,
Home is a circus, can't you see?

Each day a performance, a laugh or a grin,
At the heart of our chaos, joy thrives within.
While mice hold council, we dance 'til we tire,
In this playful kingdom, there's never a fire.

Shadows of Domestic Dreams

In every corner lurk shadows so sly,
Like dreams at daybreak, they flutter and fly.
Chasing the cat, or the roast that's gone wrong,
These are the moments that carry our song.

The laundry piles up, a mountain of clothes,
Each shirt's a story that nobody knows.
The washer's a boat, we're sailing away,
Through suds and spins, another fun day!

Coffee spills secrets as I sip too fast,
A splash on the carpet, oh, what a blast!
The echoes of laughter, both near and afar,
Bring shadows together, like bright little stars.

Every corner's a stage, each room a delight,
As we fumble through dinners and giggle all night.
In our home full of shadows, it's clear as can be,
Life's a grand circus, and we're the main spree!

Quietude in the Hushed Halls

In corners where the dust bunnies play,
Couch cushions jump into the fray.
Silent giggles echo all around,
As the cat plants paws on blankets, profound.

The clock ticks loud, it's time for tea,
While socks conspire, too wild and free.
A statue of Dad in his favorite chair,
Raising a toast to the crumbs in his hair.

Tiny hands build castles on the floor,
While the dog plans a heist to find even more.
Mopping each spill like a dance gone wrong,
In this sweet chaos, we all belong.

Mom's secret stash of cookies is near,
A fortress of flavors disappearing here.
We laugh and we bicker, but all is well,
In our world of whispers, our stories swell.

Sentinels of a Worn Threshold

The door squeaks loud, it announces the crew,
With all sorts of chaos ready to ensue.
Shoes left by the entrance, a haphazard art,
Decorating the floor, it's home's silly heart.

Each step brings a story, each floorboard, a tale,
Like the time Dad slipped, launched like a sail!
We laugh, then we sigh, at the echoes of cheer,
As the vacuum hides, full of crumbs from last year.

The hallway's a battlefield of cluttered delights,
Where action figures clash in the soft, dim lights.
Mom's apron hung like a banner of grace,
Just right for a culinary race to first place.

Grandpa's old chair, a throne of pure might,
Where stories of dragons come alive every night.
Forgive us our manners, we haven't a care,
For here tucked in laughter, we find all our fare.

Strings of Solitude and Serenity

In the nook, a lone sock takes a seat,
An untold tale of the duo's feat.
Spiders weave webs in corners of glee,
Decorating dreams, just like a spree.

The fridge hums softly, a lullaby true,
While leftovers whisper secrets anew.
The light flickers on, a dance of delight,
As shadows twist tales in the heart of the night.

Pillows become clouds, floating high and so low,
While the dog hunts dust, silent and slow.
Laughter sneaks in like a warm summer breeze,
In the sanctuary made just for our ease.

Here's to the moments, both silly and wild,
Where time is a painting, adventure compiled.
In the corners of comfort, we gather and play,
In our zipped-up laughter, we chase gloom away.

Hidden Histories of Our Haven

Underneath the stairs, old tales we find,
Of Easter egg hunts and games well designed.
The walls hold the giggles, the whispers of cheer,
A record of mischief that's sweetly sincere.

In the attic, a relic of years gone past,
A time capsule trapped in a shadowy cast.
Old toys and some books sing songs of delight,
As we rummage through memories late in the night.

The fridge is a gallery of takeout review,
Remnants of dinners that nobody knew.
Leftover tales dance through everyone's dreams,
In our homes' lasting charm, laughter redeems.

From the ceiling hangs laughter, a twinkling light,
Lighting up moments, both comedic and bright.
Nestled in chaos, it isn't a riddle,
In our patchwork of stories, we giggle and twiddle.

Fleeting Moments in the Corners

In cozy nooks where shadows dance,
A cat dives deep for a hidden chance.
The dust bunnies swirl, a furry parade,
While me and my snack try not to evade.

The couch suspects it's a pirate ship,
With cushions as treasure, a slumbering trip.
The TV keeps gossip, oh what a show,
As popcorn confetti flies high, a grand throw.!

The bathroom echoes my showering songs,
Challenging rivals with bathroom prolongs.
A rubber ducky gives a quack of cheer,
As I practice my opera, no audience here!

In every corner, a tall tale thrives,
With laughter mixed in where silliness dives.
In small spaces, joy is the treasure we find,
And these fleeting moments most lovingly bind.

Emotions Encased in Wood

The floorboards squeak with secrets untold,
As I bounce through the halls, feeling bold.
A chair creaks back, it's my trusty friend,
It knows all my quirks and the turns I take, bend.

In the kitchen, the fridge hums a tune,
While leftovers plan their escape at noon.
A spoon does a jig with the cereal bowl,
As milk plays drums, oh what a stroll!

The tablecloth flutters like a flag in a storm,
Hosting our feasts in a warm, fuzzy form.
Every scratch and stain tells a tale of its own,
As laughter and crumbs become welcome throne.

Wooden embraces that offer such warmth,
Each crevice a hug, in storm and calm form.
Here, emotions swirl, a circus of cheer,
In the daily dance of love so near.

Where Time Grows Still

In corners where clocks forget to tick,
Time takes a nap, oh what a trick!
A sunbeam lounges, sipping its tea,
While I bake a pie, just to feel free.

The family portraits wink from their frame,
Reacting to jokes that twist with the game.
Grandpa's lost glasses chill by the chair,
Pretending they're on a world tour affair!

The old vacuum whispers, 'Not today!'
Dust wars fought in a humorous play.
With socks on the ceiling, they've strayed from the floor,
Each day a surprise, who could ask for more?

In this time warp, laughter is king,
Where silliness reigns in each little thing.
Moments stand still, yet they vivify,
With joy dripping sweet like a big raspberry pie.

The Garden of Everyday Life

In the backyard, weeds wear party hats,
While squirrels hold conferences, exchanging spats.
A rogue flower blooms in a curious spot,
Claiming the pavement, a grand, silly plot!

The garden gnomes gossip 'neath sunshine beams,
While my dog plots mischief, unraveling dreams.
Sunshine and shadows play peek-a-boo,
As the hose discovers a waterfall redo!

The hammock swings low with a whispering wish,
Clouds play the saxophone, dreaming of fish.
Nature's comedians in a riot of hues,
Every leaf and petal singing their views.

Here in this garden, a circus unfolds,
With moments so silly, oh, the tales they hold.
Everyday magic sprouts bright and bold,
In laughter's embrace, see life's stories told.

www.ingramcontent.com/pod-product-compliance
Lightning Source LLC
Chambersburg PA
CBHW062107280426
43661CB00086B/275